Charles Dickens
Edgar Allan Poe
E. Nesbit

Text adapt... ...an
Illustrated by... ...olli

Editor: Efena Majomi
Design and art direction: Nadia Maestri
Computer graphics: Simona Corniola
Picture research: Laura Lagomarsino

First edition : April 2006

Picture credits:
Victoria and Albert Museum, London, UK/The Bridgeman
Art Library: 4; courtesy of Virginia State Library and
Archives: 5; Mary Evans Picture Library: 6; Library of
Congress Prints & Photographs Division, Washington, DC: 7;
Bfi Stills: 29; © Adam Woolfitt/CORBIS: 71

We would be happy to receive your comments and
suggestions, and give you any other information concerning
our material.

www.blackcat-cideb.com

CISQ CISQ CERT
TEXTBOOKS AND
TEACHING MATERIALS
The quality of the publisher's
design, production and sales processes has
been certified to the standard of
UNI EN ISO 9001

ISBN 978-88-530-0519-9   Book + CD

Printed in Italy by Litoprint, Genoa

Contents

PET Cambridge Preliminary English Test-style exercises

T: GRADE 6 Trinity-style exercises (Grade 6)

This story is recorded in full.

These symbols indicate the beginning and end of the extracts linked to the listening activities.

About the authors

Charles Dickens

Charles Dickens was born in Portsmouth in 1812. When he was ten years old, his family moved to London. But there were financial problems and his father went to prison for debt. In 1824 they sent their twelve-year-old son to work in a factory. Dickens never forgot this, and many of his novels are about the bad treatment and suffering of children.

After working as a newspaper reporter, Dickens wrote *The*

Charles Dickens (1859) by William Powell Frith.

Pickwick Papers (1836), the first of many best-selling novels that include *Oliver Twist* (1837-9), *David Copperfield* (1849-50) and *Great Expectations* (1860-1).

Dickens was interested in the supernatural, nightmares, spiritualism, the macabre [1] and the occult. He was a natural writer of ghost stories. He published these in his own weekly magazine, *Household Words* (1850-9), and later in *All the Year Round* (1859-70). The stories were

---

1. **macabre** : something strange and frightening often connected with death.

usually in the Christmas issue of the magazine because ghosts were associated with Christmas. 'The Signalman' appeared in the 1866 Christmas issue of *All the Year Round.*

A great novelist, short story writer and editor, Dickens was also a journalist, a writer of plays and hundreds of letters – and a father of ten children! He often travelled, visiting Europe and North America. He returned to America in 1867-8 to read his books in public. This was an enormous success but very hard work, and he became ill. When he died in 1870, he was very famous and was buried in Westminster Abbey.

Edgar Allan Poe

The American poet and story writer Edgar Allan Poe was born in Boston, Massachusetts, in 1809. When he was three years old, his parents died and he was adopted by John Allan, a merchant in Richmond, Virginia. From 1815 to 1820 Poe went to a private school in England. Then, in 1826, he went to the University of Virginia. He published his first book of poems in 1827. In 1831 he had to leave West

Edgar Allan Poe.

Point Military Academy because he did not do his work well. Living in Baltimore, he began to publish short stories in magazines and won a prize for 'MS [1] Found in a Bottle' (1833). He got a job as an editor in

---

1.   **MS** : manuscript, a long document written by hand.

1835 and lived with his aunt, Mrs Clemm. A year later he married his cousin Virginia, who was only thirteen years old. They moved to Richmond.

Poe lived in New York and then Philadelphia, where he continued to publish stories, including 'Ligeia' (1838) and 'The Fall of the House of Usher' (1839). During the 1840s he wrote many of his famous stories, including 'The Masque of the Red Death', 'The Black Cat' and 'The Pit and the Pendulum'.

His wife died in 1847. Poe had a nervous breakdown [1] two years later, and died of alcoholism. He has had a great influence on other writers, especially on French poets such as Baudelaire, and British writers like Robert Louis Stevenson. His story 'Murders in the Rue Morgue' (1841) made him the father of modern crime and detective fiction. Many of his horror stories have been made into films.

E. Nesbit

Edith Nesbit is famous as a writer of children's literature. Born in London in 1858, she was only three years old when her father died. She was educated in Britain, France and Germany. She married in 1880 when she was twenty-two. After working as

Edit Nesbit.

1. **nervous breakdown** : when a person becomes so sad that they cannot work or live normally.

a journalist she began to write family stories. *The Story of the Treasure Seekers* (1899), about the adventures of a group of children, was her first success.

Her most famous novel is *The Railway Children* (1906). It was very popular, but after her death in 1924 her books lost their popularity. Then they began to sell again and still sell well today. *The Railway Children* was made into a film (1970), and also adapted for television. Edith Nesbit wrote some supernatural stories, collected in *Grim Tales* (1893), *Something Wrong* (1893), and *Fear* (1910), in which 'In the Dark' first appeared.

F. Marion Crawford.

F. Marion Crawford

F. Marion Crawford was born in Italy in 1854, the son of an American sculptor. He was educated in the USA, and went to university at Cambridge and Heidelberg. He spoke many languages, and travelled widely, finding material for his novels.

His first novel, *Mr Isaacs: A Tale of Modern India*, was published in 1882 and became a best seller. He wrote almost fifty more romances, historical novels and tales of adventure. He did not write realistic or moral stories, saying that he only wanted to entertain his readers. His other novels include *Corleone: A Tale of Sicily* (1896) and *The White Sister* (1909). Many of them were adapted for the stage. In 1902 he wrote a play, *Francesca da Rimini*, for the famous actress Sarah Bernhardt.

'The Upper Berth' comes from a collection of Crawford's supernatural stories, *Wandering Ghosts* (1911), which was published after his death in 1909.

1 Answer the following questions.

1 What happened to Charles Dickens when he was twelve? What effect did this have on him?

   ....

2 What jobs did Charles Dickens have during his life?

   ....

3 Where are the various places Edgar Allan Poe lived?

   ....

4 How did Edgar Allan Poe die? What was his life like before he died?

   ....

5 Which of E. Nesbit's books was her first success?

   ....

6 Which of E. Nesbit's novels was made into a film and adapted for TV?

   ....

7 How did F. Marion Crawford find material for his novels?

   ....

8 What types of stories did F. Marion Crawford write?

   ....

The Signalman

Charles Dickens

Before you read

2 **1** **Listening**

PET

Listen to the beginning of the story and for each question, put a tick (✓) in the correct box.

1   When the narrator first called him, the signalman

   A ☐ looked up.

   B ☐ looked in the direction of the tunnel.

   C ☐ did not hear him.

2   Why did the narrator ask where the path was?

   A ☐ He wanted to go down and catch the train.

   B ☐ He wanted to go down and speak to the signalman.

   C ☐ He wanted the signalman to come up.

3   What does the narrator say about the place?

   A ☐ It was quiet, dark and lonely.

   B ☐ It had high walls and a lot of sunlight.

   C ☐ There was a red light from the sun.

4   Watching the red light

   A ☐ was not part of the signalman's job.

   B ☐ disturbed the signalman.

   C ☐ was part of the signalman's job.

5   The narrator thought the signalman

   A ☐ seemed nervous about something.

   B ☐ was probably a ghost.

   C ☐ was friendly.

6   The signalman began to relax

   A ☐ when he took the narrator to his box.

   B ☐ when the narrator said, 'I've never been there before'.

   C ☐ when the narrator pointed to the red light.

A Strange Meeting

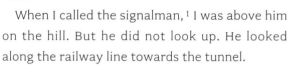

ello!'

When I called the signalman, [1] I was above him on the hill. But he did not look up. He looked along the railway line towards the tunnel.

'Hello, down there!' I called again.

Then he looked up and saw me.

'Where's the path?' I asked. 'How can I come down and speak to you?'

He did not answer me. Just then a train came out of the tunnel. The signalman had a flag in his hand and he showed it when the train passed. Again I asked him where the path was. He pointed his flag at the hill, and I saw a path that went down.

'Alright! Thanks!' I shouted.

I went down the wet path. The signalman was waiting for me at the bottom of the hill. He was standing between the railway lines with a strange, nervous expression on his face.

The place was quiet and lonely. High walls blocked out a lot of the sky, so there was not much sun there, and it was dark. I

---

1. **signalman** : the man who operates the railway signals that tell train drivers to stop or go.

looked along the line and saw a red light in front of the entrance to the black tunnel. Then I went up to the signalman, but he moved away from me. He looked at me strangely.

'It's very lonely here,' I said. 'You don't get many visitors. Am I disturbing you?'

He did not answer, but looked at the red light near the tunnel.

'Why are you watching that light?' I asked. 'Is that part of your job?'

He answered quietly, 'Don't you know it is?'

Suddenly the horrible idea came to me that he was a ghost, not a man. So I moved away. But then I saw fear in his eyes.

'Are you afraid of me?' I asked.

'I was thinking perhaps I've seen you before.'

'Where?'

He pointed to the red light. 'There.'

'Why? I've never been there before.'

'No, perhaps you haven't.'

Then he began to relax. He took me into his signal box. [1]

'Have you got much work to do here?' I asked.

'No, not very much. But I have to be very attentive and careful,' he replied.

'What are your responsibilities?'

'I change the signal, pull these switches, [2] and check that the red light is working,' he explained.

'Do you ever feel lonely?' I asked.

'No, I'm used to it.'

'Can't you ever go out into the sunlight?'

---

1. **signal box** : the cabin where a signalman works.

2. **switches** :

'Yes, sometimes when the weather is good. But I must always listen for the electric bell and watch the red light.'

I looked around his signal box. There was a fire, a desk, a telegraph machine for receiving and sending messages and a little electric bell.

'When I was a young man, I studied science,' he told me.

The bell suddenly rang. He received messages and sent replies. Then he showed his flag when a train passed. He did everything very precisely. During our conversation he opened the door twice and looked at the red light. He came back to the fire with an anxious expression. I wanted to know why, so I asked, 'Are you a happy man?'

'I was happy once,' he replied. 'But now I'm worried, sir.'

'Why? What's the problem?'

'It's difficult to say. If you come again, I'll try and tell you,' he said.

'When shall I come?'

'I'll be here again at ten o'clock tomorrow night, sir.'

'I'll come at eleven then,' I replied.

It was dark outside, so he showed me to the path with his light.

'Don't call out "hello" again, please,' he said.

'Alright.'

'And don't call out when you come tomorrow night. Why did you shout "Hello, down there!" tonight?' he asked.

'I don't know. Did I say those exact words?'

'Yes. I know those words very well.'

'I think I said them because I saw you down here,' I said.

'Is that the only reason?'

'Yes, of course. Why?'

'You don't think there was any supernatural reason?' he asked.

'No.'

Then we said goodnight, and I returned to my hotel.

Go back to the text

1 Comprehension

Answer these questions.

1 How many times did the narrator call before the signalman saw him?
2 Where was the path?
3 Why was the place dark?
4 Why did the narrator move away from the signalman?
5 What did the signalman do in his job?
6 How did the signalman behave during the conversation with the narrator?
7 What time will the narrator come tomorrow night?

2 Match the narrator's questions with the signalman's answers. Write A-F in boxes 1-6.

1 ☐ Why are you watching that red light?
2 ☐ Have you got much work to do?
3 ☐ Don't you sometimes feel lonely?
4 ☐ Are you a happy man?
5 ☐ When shall I come?
6 ☐ What's the problem?

A No, I'm used to it.
B No, not very much.
C Ten o'clock tomorrow night.
D It's difficult to say.
E Because it's part of my job.
F I was happy once.

3 Vocabulary

Look back at the text and write sentences to describe what the signalman does with these objects. Look at the example.

0 Telegraph machine   He receives and sends messages.
1 Flag   ....
2 Signal   ....
3 Switches   ....
4 Red light   ....
5 Electric bell   ....

4 Match sentences 1-6 to the correct pictures. Write 1-6 in boxes A-F.

1 I must show this when the train passes.
2 When I change this, it tells the train drivers to stop or go.
3 I always watch this because it warns of danger.
4 I use this to send and receive messages.
5 When I hear this, I know the station is calling me.
6 This is where the red light is.

5 Predicting

The signalman seems worried about something but says his problem is difficult to explain. Can you guess what the problem is? Answer the following questions using your own ideas.

1 The narrator asks, 'Why are you watching that light? Is that part of your job?' and the signalman replies, 'Don't you know it is?'
   Why does the signalman think that the narrator already knows it is part of his job?
2 The narrator asks, 'Are you afraid of me?' and the signalman replies, 'I was thinking perhaps I've seen you before.'
   So why does the signalman seem to be afraid of him?
3 'Hello, down there!' **The signalman knows the words very well. But how? Can you guess?**
4 'You don't think there was any supernatural reason?' **Why does the signalman ask this?**

16

Before you read

1 Pictures

Look at the illustration on pages 22-23.

1   Who can you see in the picture?
2   Where are they?
3   What are they doing?
4   What do you think has happened?

2 Listening

Listen to the dialogue at the beginning of Chapter Two. For each question, fill in the missing information in the numbered space.

Signalman: I've decided to tell you what disturbs me. Yesterday evening I thought (**1**) ....

Narrator: Who?

Signalman: I don't know.

Narrator: Does (**2**) .... ?

Signalman: I've never seen his face because (**3**) ....
He waves his right arm — like this.
One night (**4**) .... and I was sitting here. Suddenly
(**5**) .... — 'Hello, down there!' I went to the door
and looked out. There was somebody by (**6**) ....
the tunnel and he was waving. 'Look out! Look out!' he shouted, and
then again, 'Hello, down there! Look out!' (**7**) ....
and ran towards him. 'What's wrong? What's happened?' I called. I
wondered why he had his arm in front of his eyes. As I came near him,
I (**8**) .... to pull his arm away — but he wasn't
there.

Narrator: Did he go into the tunnel?

Signalman: No. I ran into the tunnel. I stopped and
(**9**) ...., but there was nobody there. I was scared,
(**10**) .... and came to my box.

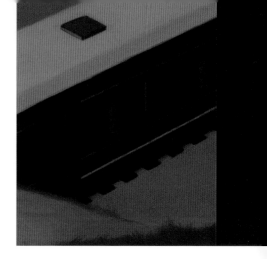

CHAPTER **TWO**

Danger

 arrived at eleven the following night. The signalman was waiting for me with his light.

'You see, I didn't call out,' I said, smiling.

We walked to the signal box and sat down by the fire.

'I've decided to tell you what disturbs me,' he began in a quiet voice. 'Yesterday evening I thought you were somebody else.'

'Who?' I asked.

'I don't know.'

'Does he look like me?'

'I've never seen his face because his left arm is always in front of it. He waves [1] his right arm — like this.' And he waved violently, like somebody trying to say, 'Please get out of the way!'

'One night,' continued the signalman, 'the moon was shining and I was sitting here. Suddenly I heard a voice — "Hello, down there!" I went to the door and looked out. There was somebody

---

1. **waves** : moves his arm from side to side.

by the red light near the tunnel and he was waving. "Look out! Look out!" he shouted, and then again, "Hello, down there! Look out!" I took my lamp and ran towards him. "What's wrong? What's happened?" I called. I wondered why he had his arm in front of his eyes. As I came near him, I put out my hand to pull his arm away — but he wasn't there.'

'Did he go into the tunnel?' I asked.

'No. I ran into the tunnel. I stopped and shone my lamp around, but there was nobody there. I was scared, so I ran out fast and came to my box. I sent a telegraph message — "Alarm received. Is anything wrong?" The answer came back: "All well."'

I said that the person was probably a hallucination. [1]

'Wait a moment, sir,' the signalman said, touching my arm. 'Six hours later a terrible accident happened on this line. They brought a lot of dead and injured people out of the tunnel.'

'But it was only a coincidence,' I said. 'A very strange coincidence.'

'Excuse me, but I haven't finished yet, sir.'

'I'm sorry,' I replied.

'This was a year ago. Six or seven months passed and I recovered from the shock. Then one morning at dawn [2] I saw the ghost again.'

'Did it call out?' I asked.

'No. It was silent.'

'Did it wave its arm?'

'No. It had its hands in front of its face — like this.' He covered his face with his hands.

---

1. **hallucination** : something you think you see but it is not real.
2. **dawn** : the time of morning when the sun comes up.

'Did you go up to it?'

'No. I came in and sat down, very frightened,' he said. 'When I went back to the door, the ghost was gone.'

'And afterwards? Did anything happen this time?' I asked again.

'Yes. That day a train came out of the tunnel, and I saw in a carriage window a lot of people standing up looking agitated. [1] I gave a signal to the driver to stop. When the train stopped, I ran to it and heard terrible screams. A beautiful young lady was dying in one of the carriages. They brought her here and put her down on the floor between us.'

I pushed back my chair in horror.

'It's true, sir. That's exactly what happened. Now listen and you'll understand why I'm worried. The ghost came back a week ago, and I've seen it again two or three times.'

'Is it always at the red light?' I asked.

'Yes, the danger light.'

'What does it do?'

'It waves — like this,' he replied. He repeated the movements that expressed the words "Please get out of the way!" Then he continued. 'I have no peace or rest. It calls me many times — "Hello, down there! Look out!" And it rings my bell.'

'Did it ring your bell yesterday when I was here?' I asked him.

'Twice,' he replied.

'Oh, it's your imagination! I was looking at the bell and listening for it, but it only rang when the station called you.'

The signalman shook his head. [2] 'No, the ghost's ring is different. You didn't see or hear it — but I did.'

---

1. **agitated** : worried and unable to think or act calmly.
2. **shook his head** : moved his head from left to right to indicate 'no'.

'And was the ghost there when you looked out?'

'Yes, twice.'

'Will you come to the door with me and look for it now?'

He came to the door and I opened it.

'Can you see it?' I asked.

'No. It's not there.'

'Right,' I said.

We went in, shut the door and sat down. Now I was certain that the ghost did not exist.

'I think you understand,' he said, 'that I'm disturbed by one question: what does the ghost mean?'

'No, I don't understand you.'

'What is the ghost warning me about? What is the danger? Where is it? Some horrible disaster is going to happen, but what can I do? I can't send a telegraph to the station. What can I say? Message: "Danger! Take care!" Answer: "What danger? Where?" Message: "Don't know. But be careful!" They'll think I'm mad.'

The poor signalman looked very worried. He pushed his fingers into his black hair. Then he took his handkerchief and wiped his face and hands.

'Why doesn't the ghost tell me where the accident will happen? Why doesn't it tell me how I can prevent it? Why didn't it say that the beautiful young lady was in danger? My God, I'm only a poor signalman! Why me!'

I tried to calm him down. I said he must do his duty well, as correctly as possible — and that was all. He became calm after a while, and I offered to stay with him for the night.

'No, it's alright, thank you,' he said. 'Come back an hour after sunset tomorrow.'

I left him at two o'clock in the morning. In my hotel room I thought about what to do. The signalman was intelligent, careful and correct in his work. But the situation disturbed him very much. How could he continue to do his job well? So I finally decided to take him to the best doctor in town.

The next evening I went out early. It was nearly sunset when I reached the path above the railway. I had another hour before the signalman came, so I decided to go for a walk. But as I looked

down at the railway I saw a man at the tunnel. He had his left arm in front of his eyes, and he was waving violently.

I cannot describe my horror. But it passed when I saw that the man was not a ghost. He was a real person, and there were some other men not far away from him. The red light was not shining. Near it was a small object like a bed covered with a sheet. I ran down the path very fast.

'What's the matter?' I asked the men.

'The signalman is dead, sir,' one of them said.

'What? The man I know?'

'If you know him, you'll recognise him.' And the man pulled back the sheet.

'Oh, how did this happen?' I cried, recognising the dead signalman.

The man at the tunnel came forward and spoke. 'A train knocked him down and killed him this morning. It was just getting light. The train came out of the tunnel, and he was standing with his lamp near the line, with his back to the train. Show the gentleman, Tom.'

'I'm the train driver, sir,' Tom said. 'I saw the signalman as I came towards the end of the tunnel. There was no time to slow down. He didn't hear my whistle, [1] so I shouted very loudly.'

'What did you say?'

'I said, "Hello, down there! Look out! Look out! Please get out of the way!" I called to him many times, and I put this arm in front of my eyes because I didn't want to see, and I waved this arm — like this — but it was too late...'

---

1. **whistle** : (here) loud noise made by the train to tell people it is coming.

Go back to the text

1 Summing it up

Put the sentences A-F in the correct order to make a summary of Chapter Two. Write 1-6 in the boxes.

A ☐ Six hours later, there was a train accident and many people died.

B ☐ The next evening the narrator saw some men at the railway tunnel.

C ☐ The signalman described how one night he saw somebody warning him at the red light.

D ☐ The train driver said he waved and shouted to warn the signalman, but it was too late — he was killed by the train!

E ☐ But the person disappeared when he came near him.

F ☐ Now the signalman was very worried because a week ago the ghost returned and warned him of danger.

2 Language

Here are some answers the signalman gives in Chapter Two. Write the questions for these answers. Look at the example.

0 A beautiful young lady.   Who _was dying on the train?_

1 At 11 p.m.   What time .... ?

2 A year ago.   When .... ?

3 Always at the red light.   Where .... ?

4 It waves — like this.   What .... ?

5 It rang twice.   How many times .... ?

PET 3 Read the text below and choose the correct word for each space. For each question, write the correct letter A, B, C or D as in the example.

The signalman looked very anxious, (0) .....B...... I told him he must continue to do his work as (1) .... as he could. That seemed to calm him down. (2) .... I said that I would stay with him for the night, he said no, (3) .... me, and asked me to come back the next day, an hour after sunset.

(4) ...., in my hotel room, I thought about the signalman's situation. It (5) .... him very much, and perhaps he would start to (6) .... mistakes in his job. In the end, I made up my (7) .... to find a doctor (8) .... could help the signalman. (9) .... who? I didn't know any doctors. (10) .... I suddenly had an idea. I said to myself, I'll take him to the best doctor in town!

0	**A** then	**B** so	**C** also	**D** that
1	**A** bad	**B** good	**C** well	**D** better
2	**A** When	**B** Why	**C** Who	**D** How
3	**A** thanked	**B** said	**C** looked	**D** told
4	**A** After	**B** Before	**C** Later	**D** Sooner
5	**A** worried	**B** pleased	**C** liked	**D** helped
6	**A** do	**B** make	**C** have	**D** cause
7	**A** idea	**B** mind	**C** head	**D** decision
8	**A** who	**B** what	**C** how	**D** whose
9	**A** So	**B** And	**C** As	**D** But
10	**A** Because	**B** When	**C** Then	**D** As

'I've never seen his face'

The Present Perfect Simple is formed with **has/have + the past participle** of the main verb. We often use it to describe a period of time that continues from the past until the present.

Compare it with this sentence:
*When the ghost **appeared** a week ago, I **didn't see** his face.*

Here the speaker is speaking about a completed action at a specific time in the past, so he uses the Past Simple.

We often use the Present Perfect with adverbs such as *never, ever* and *yet*.

Note that **ever** is used in questions: *Have you **ever** seen his face?*

Yet is used to mean 'until now' and is only used in questions and negatives: *Have you finished **yet**?*
*Excuse me, but I haven't finished **yet**.*

4 The Present Perfect

Complete the sentences with the verbs provided, using the Present Perfect Simple or the Past Simple. Where necessary choose *never, ever* or *yet*.

1 I .... *(think)* a lot about your question and now I'll give you an answer.

2 .... you *(never/ever/yet)* .... *(see)* a ghost?

3 When the ghost rang the bell, you .... *(not hear)* it.

4 The ghost .... *(come)* back a week ago, and it .... *(appear)* again two or three times.

5 .... the signalman .... *(change)* the signal *(never/ever/yet?)*.

6 .... the ghost .... *(ring)* the bell when I .... *(be)* here yesterday?

7 The signalman does not know where the accident will happen because the ghost .... *(not tell)* him *(never/ever/yet)*.

8 The signalman thinks he recognises the narrator, but the narrator says this is not possible because he .... *(never/ever/yet)* .... *(be)* there before.

5 Write about it

Write a story in about 100 words that includes the following words:

ghost	hand	bus/plane	beautiful lady	station/airport

....

....

....

....

....

....

....

....

The Supernatural
in English Literature

The supernatural describes things that we cannot explain scientifically. It includes the occult, magic, magical forces and mysticism. Many famous English writers have used the supernatural in their novels, stories, and plays. In Shakespeare's *Hamlet*, for example, the ghost of Hamlet's father appears to his son and describes how Claudius, his brother and Hamlet's uncle, murdered him. In Emily Brontë's novel *Wuthering Heights* (1847) the ghost of Catherine Earnshaw haunts [1] Heathcliff and appears to the narrator Lockwood, who thinks he is dreaming when he sees her trying to get into his room through a broken window.

The supernatural first appeared in fiction in 1764 in the gothic tale *The Castle of Otranto* by Horace Walpole (1717-97). He was the youngest son of the first British prime minister Sir Robert Walpole. He was a Member of Parliament but also wrote. His famous horror story set in the Middle Ages, started the fashion for gothic romances. These romances describe strange or mysterious adventures that take place in dark and lonely places.

By the 19th century gothic stories were very popular. Mary Shelley's *Frankenstein* (1818) is still one of the most important gothic horror stories, and continues to frighten readers today. But the modern ghost story began to appear in Victorian times after 1837. Charles Dickens wrote the most famous ghost story of all, *A Christmas Carol*

---

1. **haunts** : (used of a ghost) visits a person or a place regularly.

A scene from the film **The Innocents** (1961).

(1843). It is a moral story in which various ghosts help the mean [1] protagonist Scrooge to change his life.

Hundreds of ghost stories were published from 1850 to the early twentieth century. The years 1890-1940 were the golden age of this popular form of short fiction. These stories reflected people's fascination with death and the uncertainty of what happens after we die. Many important writers also wrote ghost stories during this time. They include Rudyard Kipling, famous for *The Jungle Book*, and R. L. Stevenson, who wrote *Treasure Island*. The great novelist Henry James also published many supernatural tales. His masterpiece, *The Turn of the Screw* (1898), was made into a film called *The Innocents* in 1961. Other famous ghost story writers are Bram Stoker, author of

---

1. **mean** : if you are mean you do not like to spend money.

Dracula (1897), H. G. Wells, and the Americans Nathaniel Hawthorne, who wrote the supernatural thriller *The House of Green Gables* (1851), and Edith Wharton. The stories in her collection *Tales of Men and Ghosts* were published individually in magazines from 1909-10.

Some writers were specialists in the genre. The American H. P. Lovecraft (1890-1937), who wrote *The Dunwich Horror* (1945), has become a cult figure. The English scholar M. R. James (1862-1936) is considered a master of the ghost story, and he has had a great influence on other writers.

Tales of the supernatural are still popular today. Contemporary fiction such as *The Woman in Black* (1983) by Susan Hill became a best seller, and then a successful play. Books by modern gothic authors such as Stephen King and Anne Rice are worldwide best sellers.

1 Are these sentences true (T) or false (F)? Correct the false ones.

		T	F
1	In Shakespeare's play the ghost of Hamlet's father tells his son how he died.	☐	☐
2	In *Wuthering Heights* Catherine Earnshaw's ghost haunts the room of the narrator Lockwood.	☐	☐
3	The supernatural first appeared in stories in the 18th century.	☐	☐
4	The modern ghost story began to appear in Victorian times.	☐	☐
5	Supernatural stories were popular because people were frightened of death.	☐	☐
6	*The Jungle Book* is a famous supernatural story.	☐	☐
7	Important novelists never wrote about the supernatural.	☐	☐
8	The supernatural did not interest American writers.	☐	☐
9	Some writers specialised in ghost stories.	☐	☐
10	*The Woman in Black* was adapted for the theatre.	☐	☐

Ligeia

Edgar Allan **Poe**

Before you read

1 **Listening**

PET Listen to the beginning of the story and for each question, put a tick (✓) in the correct box.

1 What does the narrator remember well about Ligeia?

   A ☐ her family name

   B ☐ her physical appearance

   C ☐ the city where he first met her

2 The narrator never heard Ligeia coming into his studio because

   A ☐ she was aristocratic.

   B ☐ she did not speak.

   C ☐ her footsteps were very soft.

3 What was strange about Ligeia's beauty?

   A ☐ her long nose and red mouth

   B ☐ the expression in her eyes

   C ☐ her white skin and black hair

4 Ligeia's determination

   A ☐ shone in her eyes.

   B ☐ showed in her clever mind.

   C ☐ helped her in her studies.

5 The expression in Ligeia's eyes

   A ☐ fascinated and sometimes frightened the narrator.

   B ☐ was terrible.

   C ☐ was always calm and quiet.

6 After Ligeia died the narrator

   A ☐ was frightened of the dark.

   B ☐ did not study any more.

   C ☐ was lonely and insecure.

A Beautiful Wife

cannot remember how, when or where I met Ligeia. It was a long time ago and my memory is not good. But I think I met her first in a large, old city near the Rhine in Germany.

She told me that she came from an ancient family. But I never knew the family name of the woman who was my friend, my partner in my studies and finally my wife. Why did I never discover her family name? Perhaps because she did not want me to find out, but I cannot remember.

I remember one thing very well: Ligeia was tall and slim. Later, at the end, she became very thin. How can I describe her quiet, aristocratic movements, or the strange softness of her footsteps? [1] If she came into my office, I only knew she was there

---

1. **footsteps** : the sound made by a person walking.

when I heard her voice, or when she put her white hand on my shoulder.

She had a beautiful face, but it was not a classical kind of beauty. There was something strange about it. I have often tried to understand it: was it her pure white skin or her thick, black hair? I looked at her long, delicate nose many times. It was perfect! I looked at her sweet mouth. How soft and red it was! And when she smiled, her teeth were white. Then I looked into her eyes.

They were much bigger than normal eyes. Sometimes, when she was excited, they looked like a deer's [1] eyes. They were black, with long black eyelashes and black eyebrows. But as I looked into them, I realised that they had a strange expression. I thought about it for many hours, sometimes all night. What *was* the expression in those eyes? I wanted to know. Many times I thought I almost had the answer, but then it was gone.

Ligeia was very determined. She was always calm and quiet, but her determination showed in her eyes. It shone like a terrible energy, and sometimes it frightened me.

Ligeia was very clever. She was excellent at Latin and Greek, and she knew many other languages perfectly; she never made a mistake. She was also a student of science and mathematics. When we were first married I often asked her for help with my studies, and we worked together. But after she died I was alone. Without her I was like a child in the dark.

When she first became ill, she did not come to help me as often as before. She lost weight and her skin became pale and

1. deer :

transparent. When I saw that she was dying, I felt desperate. Ligeia resisted death with all her energy — she was determined to live. I watched in agony as she fought for life.

I knew she loved me, but I only understood how much she loved me now that she was dying. She held my hands and said that she was devoted to me. I cannot talk about it now, but let me say that her love for me was part of her determination to live. On the night she died she suddenly got out of bed and cried, 'Oh God, must I die? Must I lose my fight with death? No, I can't die like this!'

But my dear Ligeia died. I was so sad I could not stay in the old city by the Rhine. For a few months I travelled around, then I bought an old abbey 1 in an isolated part of England. This dark, sad place expressed my feelings of loneliness. But I decorated it with beautifully coloured curtains, carpets and ornaments. I said to myself, 'Perhaps the bright colours will make me feel happier.' Unfortunately they did not. I began to drink too much. But I do not want to speak about that time of my life. I will only say that one day I married Lady Rowena Trevanion of Tremaine. My new wife had blonde hair and blue eyes. She was very different from my first wife, but how could I ever forget Ligeia?

---

1. **abbey** : church with buildings where religious communities of men or women live. Here, the abbey is no longer used for religious purposes.

Go back to the text

1 Comprehension

Answer these questions.

1 Why can't the narrator say how, when, or where he met Ligeia?
2 How did the narrator know when Ligeia was in his studio?
3 What did the narrator want to know about Ligeia?
4 Describe briefly what kind of student Ligeia was.
5 How did Ligeia change physically when she first became ill?
6 When did the narrator understand how much Ligeia loved him?
7 Why was Ligeia determined to live?
8 Where did the narrator go to live after Ligeia died?
9 Why did the narrator begin to drink too much?
10 How was Lady Rowena physically different from Ligeia?

2 Can you remember what happened in these places? Write a sentence under each picture.

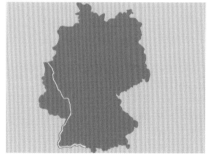

1 ....

2 ....

3 ....

4 ....

3 Complete the sentences with the correct word from the box.

> transparent   slim   delicate   eyelashes   quiet
> determination   lonely   softness   scientific   calm   sad   pale

1   Ligeia studied .... subjects, like chemistry.
2   The .... in Ligeia's eyes sometimes frightened the
    narrator.
3   Ligeia had long, black .... and a long,
    .... nose.
4   When Ligeia was ill, her skin changed. It became ....
    and ....
5   Ligeia's footsteps had a strange ....
6   Ligeia was very determined, but she always seemed
    .... and ....
7   Before her illness Ligeia was not thin. She was ....
8   When Ligeia died, the narrator felt .... and
    ....

4 The narrator and his second wife Rowena are talking about Ligeia.
Read the dialogue and complete the narrator's part.

Rowena: When did you meet your first wife, dear?
Narrator: [1]...
Rowena: Really? That's strange. What was the name of her family?
Narrator: [2]...
Rowena: Don't you remember *anything* about her?
Narrator: I remember one thing well. [3]...
....
Rowena: What did she look like?
Narrator: [4] ....

Rowena: Hmm. So she was very beautiful in your opinion?

Narrator. Yes, but [5]...

Rowena: Strange? How?

Narrator: Well, her eyes had [6].. .
It sometimes frightened me

Rowena: Oh, really? But what about her mind? Was she clever?

Narrator: [7].. .
She never made a mistake.

Rowena: Oh, you think Ligeia was so beautiful and clever! Now I understand why you're always sad. You think about her all the time. You're still in love with her — aren't you?

Compare your answers with a partner.

◆ PET **5** Writing

Here is part of a letter you receive from a penfriend.

Films about horror and the supernatural are my favourite type of films. In your next letter, please tell me about your favourite films. Why do you like them?

Write a letter of about 100 words answering your penfriend's question.

....
....
....
....
....
....

Before you read

1 Pictures

Look at the illustration on page 45 with a partner. Take turns to describe what you can see and discuss what you think is happening.

2 Listening

Listen to the beginning of Chapter Two and decide if each sentence is correct or incorrect. If it is correct, put a tick (✓) in the box under A for YES. If it is not correct, put a tick (✓) in the box under B for NO.

		A YES	B NO
1	After their marriage the narrator and Rowena lived in a large room at the top of a tower.	☐	☐
2	The room had a high ceiling and no windows.	☐	☐
3	Lady Rowena was afraid of the narrator.	☐	☐
4	The narrator and his wife spent a lot of time together.	☐	☐
5	The narrator could not forget Ligeia.	☐	☐
6	Lady Rowena became ill in the second month of their marriage.	☐	☐
7	At first the narrator did not believe that Rowena could hear sounds and movements in the tower.	☐	☐
8	Rowena's second illness was not as bad as the first.	☐	☐
9	There was some wine on the table next to the bed.	☐	☐
10	The narrator told Rowena that there was a shadow on the carpet.	☐	☐

CHAPTER **TWO**

A Fight with Death

I took Lady Rowena back to a room high up in the tower of the abbey, where we lived for the first month of our marriage. The room was very large, with an enormous window made of glass from Venice. The ceiling was high, like a church, and in the centre there was a big gold chandelier. [1] There were sofas from the East, and an Indian bed. On the walls were long tapestries, [2] like carpets, with designs made of gold. The tapestries moved every time the wind blew.

My wife was afraid of me because I was often sad and depressed. She did not love me much and stayed away from me, but I preferred this. I always thought about Ligeia — my beautiful, Ligeia, dead in the tomb. Sometimes in my dreams I called to her in the night. I imagined that perhaps my love for her could bring her back to me.

1. chandelier :   2. tapestries :

At the beginning of the second month Lady Rowena became ill. She did not sleep very well, and told me she could hear sounds and movements in the tower.

'You have a fever,' I said. 'You're imagining things.'

She got better, but then she went back to bed with a second illness, worse than the first. The doctors could not understand it. Again Rowena began to hear little sounds and movements in the bedroom, and they frightened her.

One night at the end of September she woke up suddenly. I was sitting on a sofa by her bed. She whispered to me that she could hear sounds and see movements, and there was a frightened expression on her thin face. But I saw and heard nothing.

'It's the wind,' I explained. 'You can see the tapestries moving in the wind.'

But her face was white with fear, and she nearly fainted.[1] I remembered that there was some wine on the table on the other side of the room. As I walked under the light of the chandelier, a strange thing happened. I felt something invisible pass me, and on the carpet I saw a shadow, almost the shadow of a shadow. I decided to say nothing to Rowena.

I poured out a glass of wine and gave it to her. Then I sat on the sofa and watched her. After some moments I heard very quiet footsteps on the carpet, coming towards the bed. A second later, as Rowena was about to drink the wine, I saw — or perhaps I dreamed that I saw — three or four large drops of a bright red liquid fall into the glass. Rowena did not see it; she drank the wine, and I said nothing because I thought it was only my imagination.

1. **fainted** : lost consciousness.

After this, Rowena's health got much worse, and on the third night she died. Her servants prepared her for the tomb, then covered her with a sheet. The next night I sat alone with her body in the bedroom. Strange forms and shadows moved around me. I looked nervously into the dark corners, at the moving tapestries, and I felt frightened.

Then I looked at the carpet under the chandelier. There was no shadow there, and I felt better. When I looked at Rowena on the bed, sad memories of Ligeia — the only woman I ever loved — came back to me.

It was perhaps around midnight when I heard a sound. It was quiet but clear, and it woke me from my dreams. I thought it came from the bed. I listened in terror, but I did not hear it again. I looked carefully at Rowena for any sign of life. She was not moving, but I continued to look at her.

Minutes passed. Then I noticed a little colour in Rowena's face. My heart stopped in horror; I could not move. When I understood that Rowena was not dead, I tried to revive her. [1] But soon the colour disappeared from her cheeks, her face looked like marble again and her lips were thin with the horrible expression of death. When her body was cold and rigid, I fell on to the sofa and dreamed about Ligeia.

An hour later I heard the same sound as before. I listened; yes, there it was again — a sigh [2] from the bed! I ran over and saw clearly that her lips were trembling. Then they opened, showing her bright teeth. I thought I was going mad. There was a pink colour on her cheeks and neck, her body was getting warm

1. **revive her** : bring her back to life.
2. **sigh** : a long, quiet breathing sound.

again and her heart was beating a little. Lady Rowena was alive!

I did everything I could to revive her. Then suddenly her colour disappeared, her heart stopped and her body became cold and rigid. I sat down and began to think about Ligeia again. Then again for the third time there was a sound from the bed. But why must I describe the horrors of that night? Again I tried to revive Rowena, and then a fourth time. Each time she seemed to fight with an invisible force; and each time her body changed. I cannot say how, but she looked different.

It was nearly dawn when she moved again. I was sitting on the sofa, exhausted, but Rowena's body moved with more energy than before. Her colour returned, signs of life changed her face. Her eyes were closed, but she looked alive. Then she suddenly got out of bed and walked slowly to the centre of the room, like she was walking in her sleep.

I did not tremble; I did not move. I was as cold and still as stone, paralysed [1] by what I saw. As I looked at her, my head filled with wild thoughts. Was Rowena really alive? Could I really see her blonde hair and blue eyes? Why wasn't I certain? I could not see her mouth very well, but her cheeks were like pink roses. Weren't they Rowena's cheeks? *But wasn't she taller than before?*

I was filled with a kind of madness. I ran to her, but she moved away. Then I saw her long hair moving in the wind — it was blacker than the black of midnight! And now slowly her eyes opened.

I shouted like a madman, 'These are the black eyes of my lost love — the eyes of Ligeia!'

---

1. **paralysed** : not able to move.

Go back to the text

1 Comprehension

Choose the correct picture (A, B or C).

1 When did the narrator hear the first sound from the bed?

A ☐   B ☐   C ☐

2 Approximately when did the narrator first notice a little colour in Rowena's face?

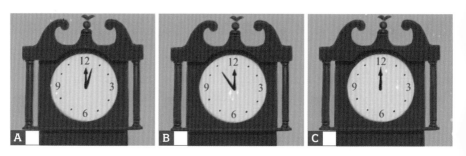

A ☐   B ☐   C ☐

3 What happened an hour later?

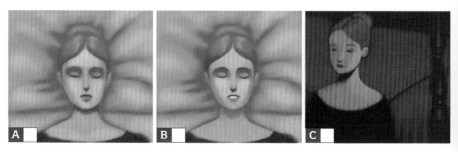

A ☐   B ☐   C ☐

4   When did Rowena get out of bed?

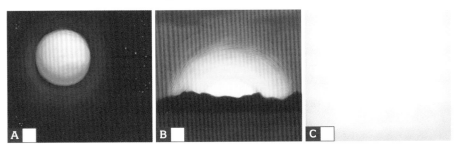

2 Language

Complete the sentences with the words in brackets in their correct form, as in the example.

1   There was an ..Indian............ bed in the room. *(India)*
2   The tapestries moved when it was .... *(wind)*
3   Rowena went back to bed with a second .... *(ill)*
4   I thought it was only my .... , so I said nothing. *(image)*
5   Then for the .... time there was a sound from the bed. *(three)*
6   At the .... of the second month Lady Rowena became ill. *(begin)*
7   We lived in the room during the first month of our .... *(marry)*
8   Lady Rowena said she heard sounds and saw .... in the tower. *(move)*
9   I was filled with a kind of .... *(mad)*

3 Your opinion

- Why do you think the narrator remarried even though he could not forget his first wife, Ligeia?
- Do you think Ligeia was really 'reborn', or is the narrator mad?
- Have you had any supernatural experiences? (ghosts, fortune tellers, etc.) Where were you and what happened?

Discuss your ideas with a partner.

INTERNET PROJECT

Connect to the Internet and go to www.blackcat-cideb.com or www.cideb.it. Insert the title or part of the title of the book into our search engine. Open the page for *Tales of the Supernatural*. Click on the Internet project link. Go down the page until you find the title of this book and click on the relevant link for this project.

Find out about the many adaptations of Poe's short stories. Look for the following:

'The Pit and the Pendulum'   'The Masque of the Red Death'

'Ligeia'   'The Murders in the Rue Morgue'

'The Fall of the House of Usher'

▶ Find out the names of the film directors and actors. When were the films made? Can you find more films of Poe's stories?

▶ Poe was also a poet. What can you discover about a poem called 'The Raven'?

▶ Organise your class into two groups. Each group can report to the class on **one** of the following:

Horror films based on Poe's stories.

'The Raven' – a poem by Edgar Allan Poe.

T: GRADE 6

4 Speaking

Topic — Health

Poe does not tell us much about Ligeia's illness, but in the 19th century people often died young of diseases like tuberculosis. Today advances in medical science and hygiene have changed this situation in many countries. Find some information or pictures showing how modern knowledge can help us to live a long and healthy life. Think about the following:

diet   smoking   exercise

hygiene   free health service

• Can you think of some dangers to health today?

• What can governments and the media do to educate people about health?

• What sort of things do *you* do to keep healthy?

In the Dark

E. Nesbit

Before you read

1 **Pictures**

Look at the illustration on page 55.

1   What can you see?

2   What do you think happened before?

2 **Listening**

Listen to the beginning of the story and decide if each sentence is correct or incorrect. If it is correct, put a tick (✓) in the box under A for YES. If it is not correct, put a tick (✓) in the box under B for NO.

		A YES	B NO
1	Haldane and the narrator did not like Visger.	☐	☐
2	Visger knew that Haldane and Winston stole the cherries.	☐	☐
3	At school and university Haldane was a miserable person.	☐	☐
4	When the narrator visited him, Haldane seemed a different person.	☐	☐
5	When the narrator arrived Haldane was packing his things.	☐	☐
6	The two friends had dinner in a restaurant.	☐	☐
7	Haldane laughed a lot at the narrator's jokes during dinner.	☐	☐
8	The narrator thought that something was wrong with Haldane.	☐	☐
9	Haldane did not want to be the narrator's friend.	☐	☐
10	The narrator spent the night at Haldane's house.	☐	☐

CHAPTER **ONE**

A Shocking Confession

Maybe he was mad. Maybe he had a sixth sense.
Or was he really haunted? [1] He told me the first
part of the story, and I saw the last part with
my own eyes.

At school my friend Haldane and I hated a boy called Visger.
When we did something wrong, he always told the teacher. One
day we stole some cherries [2] from a tree.

'Do you know who did it, Visger?' the teacher asked.

'It was Haldane and Winston,' he replied.

Later, Haldane asked him how he knew it was us.

'I didn't know,' he said. 'I just felt certain. And I was right.'

Haldane and I grew up. Visger became a vegetarian and never
drank alcohol. He also became Sir George Visger.

---

1. **haunted** : visited by the ghost of a dead person.

2. **cherries** :

When we all left Oxford University, I went away to India. After a year I came back and wanted to see Haldane. He was always happy, kind, and honest. I wanted to see the smile in his blue eyes again and hear his happy laugh, so I went to visit him in London. But this time he did not laugh. He was miserable, his face was pale and he looked weak and ill.

He was packing his things, and there were lots of big boxes full of furniture and books around the house.

'I'm moving,' he said. 'I don't like this house. There's something strange about it; I'm going tomorrow.'

'Let's go out and have some dinner,' I said.

'I'm too busy.' He looked nervously around the room. 'Look, I'm really happy to see you, but... Why don't you go to the restaurant and bring back some food?'

When I came back, we sat by the fire and ate the food. I tried to tell jokes and he tried to laugh, but sometimes he looked into the shadows in the corners of the room. We finished our meal, and then I said, 'Well?'

'What's the matter?'

'You tell *me*,' I answered.

He was silent. Again he looked into the shadows.

'You're very nervous,' I said. 'What is it? Drink? Gambling? [1] Women? Tell me, or go and tell your doctor. You're ill, my friend.'

'I won't be your friend if you talk like that.'

'Well, I *am* your friend, and something is wrong. Come on, tell me.'

But he did not tell me anything. He asked me to stay for the

---

1. **gambling** : winning or losing money in a game or race.

night, but I had a room in a hotel so I left him. When I returned the next morning, he was gone and some men were putting his boxes into a van. [1] Haldane did not leave his new address.

I saw him again more than a year later. He came to see me early one morning before breakfast. He looked really bad, worse than before. His face was thin and white, like a ghost, and his hands were shaking.

I invited him to have breakfast with me, but I did not ask him any questions because I knew he wanted to tell me something. I made coffee, talked and waited.

'I'm going to kill myself,' he began. 'Don't worry, I won't do it here or now. I'll do it when it's necessary, when I can't continue to live any more. And I want somebody to know why. Can I tell you?'

'Yes, of course,' I said, astonished.' [2]

'You must promise not to tell anybody while I'm alive,' he said.

'I promise.'

He looked at the fire silently. 'It's difficult to begin,' he said. 'You remember George Visger, don't you?'

'Yes. I haven't seen him for a long time, but somebody told me he went to an island to teach vegetarianism to the cannibals.' I laughed. 'Anyway, he's gone.'

Haldane did not laugh. 'Yes, he's gone. But not to an island. He's dead.'

'Dead? How?'

---

1. **van** : a large vehicle that is used to transport things.
2. **astonished** : very surprised.

'You remember he always *knew* when people did bad things, and told the teacher? Well, he told a girl some bad things about me. I loved her, but she left me. Then she died suddenly — oh, it was terrible! When I went to the funeral, he was there. I came back home and sat thinking about it, and then he arrived.'

'I hope you told him to go away,' I said angrily.

'No. I listened to him. He came to say it was better that she was dead and we hadn't got married. I asked why and he said because there was madness in my family.'

'And is there?'

'I don't know, but he said he knew and had told my girlfriend. I said I never knew anything about madness in the family. And he said, "So, you see, it's better you didn't get married, isn't it?" And then I put my hands round his neck. I don't know if I meant to kill him, but that's what happened.'

I was shocked. I said nothing; what can you say when your friend tells you he is a murderer?

Haldane continued. 'I saw that he was dead, but I was very calm. I sat down and thought, there's no blood, no weapon. [1] Everybody knows Visger is going to an island, and he told me he's said goodbye to them. So there's no problem; I must get rid of [2] his body, that's all.'

'How?'

He smiled. 'No, I won't tell you. You promised not to tell anybody, but maybe you'll talk in your sleep or when you have a fever one day. I'll be safe if you don't know where the body is, do you see?'

---

1. **weapon** : something used for attack or defence, e.g. a gun.
2. **get rid of** : free yourself from something that you do not want.

I was sorry for my friend, but I could not believe he was a murderer.

I said, 'Yes, I see. Look, let's go away together. Let's travel and see the world, and forget about Visger.'

He looked very happy. 'You understand and you don't hate me! Why didn't I tell you before? It's too late now.'

'Too late? No, it isn't. Come on, we'll pack our suitcases tonight. We'll go where nobody can find us.'

He said, 'When I tell you what has happened to me, you'll change your mind.'

'But I know what has happened to you.'

'No,' he said slowly, 'I've told you what happened to *him*, not what happened to me. That's very different. Did I tell you what his last words were? Just before I put my hands around his neck he said, "Careful, Haldane! You'll never get rid of my body." Well, I got rid of his body, and I forgot about his last words. But a year later I was sitting here and I suddenly remembered them. "I got rid of your body very easily, Visger!" I said. And then I looked at the carpet in front of the fire and — Aaah!' Haldane screamed very loudly. 'I can't tell you — no, I can't!'

Go back to the text

1 Summing it up

Match the first half of each sentence (A-G) with the second half (1-7) to make a summary of Chapter One. Write 1-7 in the boxes.

A ☐ At school Haldane and the narrator hated Visger because
B ☐ A year after they left Oxford, the narrator went to visit Haldane
C ☐ When the narrator asked him what was wrong
D ☐ Over a year later Haldane came to the narrator's rooms
E ☐ Then Haldane confessed to Visger's murder
F ☐ The narrator did not believe Haldane and suggested
G ☐ But Haldane said it was too late, and told him that Visger's last words were,

1 and told him he was going to kill himself.
2 'You'll never get rid of the body.'
3 he always told the teacher when they did something wrong.
4 but did not want to say where Visger's body was.
5 Haldane did not tell him anything.
6 and saw that he was nervous and unhappy.
7 that they could go away that night and travel.

PET 2 Language

Here are five sentences from the story. For each question, complete the second sentence so that it means the same as the first. Use no more than three words.

0 'It's difficult to begin,' Haldane said.
'It's ....*not easy*.................... to begin,' Haldane said.

1 I saw Haldane again more than a year later.
I .... Haldane again for more than a year.

2 There's something strange about these rooms.
These rooms .... something strange about them.

3 Haldane asked Visger how he knew it was them.
'How .... it was us?' Haldane asked Visger.

4 'I haven't seen Visger for a long time,' I said.
   'It's a long time since .... Visger,' I said.

T: GRADE 6

3 Speaking

Topic — Travel

'Let's travel and see the world,' says the narrator. Do you like travelling? If so, what do you like about it? Is there anything you do not like? Find some information or pictures to show the different reasons why people travel. Think about the following ideas:

- types of holidays (beach, sun, etc.)
- discovering new lifestyles, cultures, food, etc.
- visiting famous places
- sports and activities (mountain climbing, skiing, scuba diving, etc.)
- adventure (backpacking, trekking, etc.)

Before you read

1 Predicting

Before you continue, try to guess why Haldane screams and says, 'I can't tell you!' What did he see on the carpet?

2 Listening

Listen to the beginning of Chapter Two and for each question, tick (✓) the correct picture.

1 What was the weather like?

A ☐   B ☐   C ☐

2   What did Haldane see in his room?

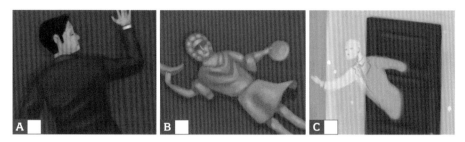

3   Where did Haldane see the body again?

4   How did Haldane feel after travelling for a month or two?

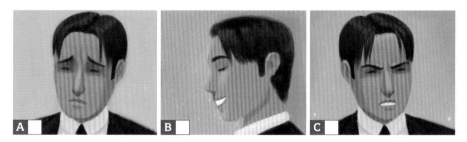

5   Where did the narrator sleep in the hotel room in Bruges?

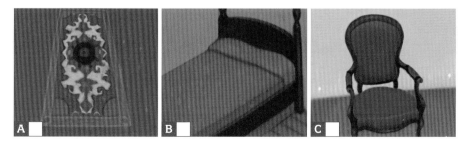

CHAPTER **TWO**

A Haunted Man

 t that moment we heard thunder [1] outside. I went to the window and saw some dark storm clouds in the sky.

'Where was I?' Haldane said. 'Oh yes. I looked at the carpet and there *he* was — Visger. I can't explain it: the door was closed, the windows were closed. He wasn't there before, and he was there now. That's all.'

'A hallucination,' I said.

'That's exactly what I thought,' he answered. 'But I touched it. It was real; it was heavy and hard, like stone. The arms were rigid like the arms of a statue.'

'It was a hallucination,' I repeated.

'Well, I thought somebody had put him here to frighten me, so I went to the place where I had hidden him, and he was there, just as he was a year before.'

---

1. **thunder** : the loud sound that you hear from the sky during a storm.

'My dear Haldane,' I said, 'this is very funny.'

'You might think it's funny, but when I wake up in the night and think of it, it isn't funny at all. I don't want to die in the dark, Winston. That's why I think I'll kill myself, so I'm sure that I won't die in the dark.'

'Is that all?'

'No, he came back again. I was asleep on the train one day, and when I woke up, he was on the seat opposite me. He looked the same as before, hard and rigid like a statue. I threw him out of the window in a tunnel. If I see him again, I'll kill myself. You think I'm mad, but I'm not. You can't help me, nobody can help me. He *knew*, you see? He said, "You'll never get rid of my body," and I can't. He always knew things. Winston, I promise you I'm not mad.'

'I don't think you're mad; I think your mind is disturbed. But we'll stay together; if you can talk to me, you won't imagine things.'

So we went travelling together, and I was full of hope. Haldane was always a rational man, and I could not believe he was mad. I wanted to help him get better. After a month or two the 'madness' passed and we joked and laughed again. I was extremely happy that my old friend was normal. 'He's forgotten about Visger,' I thought, 'and now he's fine!'

We arrived in Bruges, where there was a big exhibition and all the hotels were full. We could only find one room with a single bed in a hotel called the Grande Vigne, so I had to sleep in the armchair.

We had dinner and went to a pub, and it was late when we returned to our room. We talked for a while, and then Haldane got into bed. I tried to sleep in the armchair, but it was not very comfortable. I was nearly asleep when Haldane began to talk about his will. [1]

'I've left everything to you, Winston,' he said. 'I know I can trust you to take care of everything.'

'Thank you,' I said sleepily. 'Let's talk about it in the morning.'

But he continued, telling me what a good friend I was. I told him to go to sleep, but he said he was thirsty.

'Oh, alright,' I said. 'Light the candle and go and get some water — and then please let me sleep!'

'No, you light it. I don't want to get out of bed in the dark. I might step on something or walk into something that wasn't there when I got into bed.'

I lit the candle, and he sat up in bed and looked at me. His face was very pale, his hair untidy and his eyes were shining.

'That's better,' he said. 'Oh, look here! There are two big letters on the sheet in red cotton. GV! George Visger!'

'No, it's the symbol of the Hotel Grande Vigne,' I said. 'Hurry up and get the water!'

'Please come with me, Winston.'

'I'll go down by myself.' And I went to the door with the candle in my hand. He jumped off the bed in a second.

'No! I don't want to stay alone in the dark,' he said like a frightened child.

I tried to make a joke of it, but I was very disappointed. It was clear to me that all my time spent trying to help him had been

---

1. **will** : legal document that says who will have your money and property when you die.

wasted, and that he was not better after all. We went down as quietly as we could, and got some water from the dining room. Haldane took the candle from me, and went very slowly back towards our room. He looked around very carefully. I knew what he was looking for, and I became angry and nervous. When we entered the room, I almost expected to see something on the carpet, but of course there was nothing. I put out the candle, pulled the blankets [1] round me, and tried to get comfortable in my chair so I could sleep again.

'You've got all the blankets,' Haldane said.

'No, I haven't. Only the ones I had before.'

'Well, I can't find mine. I'm so cold. Light the candle! Quick, light it! There's something horrible...'

But I could not find the matches.

'Light the candle, light the candle!' he shouted. 'If you don't, he'll come to me, he'll come in the dark. I can't die in the dark; please, Winston, light the candle!'

'I *am* lighting it,' I said angrily. But in the dark I was trying to find the matches with my hands — on the shelf, the table... I could not remember where I had put them. 'You're not going to die. It's alright. I'll get the matches in a second.'

'It's cold. It's cold. It's cold,' he said, like that, three times. And then he screamed loudly, like a child, or like a rabbit attacked by dogs.

'What is it?' I cried.

There was silence. Then, very slowly, 'It's Visger,' he said, and his voice seemed strange and distant.

---

1. **blankets** :

'Of course it isn't!' My hand found the matches as I spoke.

'He's here!' he screamed. 'Here, next to me. In the bed.'

I lit the candle. I ran to the bed.

He was lying on the edge of the bed. Next to him was a dead man, white and cold.

Haldane had died in the dark.

***

There was a simple explanation. Haldane and I were in the wrong room — the dead man's room. His name was Felix Leblanc, and he had died from a heart attack earlier that day.

I found out more information in England. The police found the body of a man with a bottle of poison in his hand in a railway tunnel. His name was Simmons, and he had drunk poison in Haldane's carriage because he was depressed. Haldane had thrown his body out of the window.

Haldane left me all his possessions in his will. I asked a police inspector to be with me when I opened the boxes he had left me. Inside one were the bodies of two men. One man was identified later; he was a salesman who had died of epilepsy. The other body was Visger's.

I leave it to you to explain the events in this story. I cannot find an explanation that satisfies me.

Go back to the text

PET **1** Comprehension

Read the questions below and for each question, choose the correct answer (A, B, C or D).

1 In the narrator's opinion, Haldane
   A ☐ saw Visger's body.
   B ☐ did not see anything.
   C ☐ imagined that he saw Visger's body.
   D ☐ was not telling the truth.

2 Haldane decided that he would kill himself
   A ☐ one night.
   B ☐ if he saw Visger's body again.
   C ☐ today.
   D ☐ because he thought he was mad.

3 In the hotel Haldane did not want to be alone because
   A ☐ there was no light.
   B ☐ he was thirsty.
   C ☐ he did not trust the narrator.
   D ☐ he was afraid of seeing Visger's body again.

4 Haldane died
   A ☐ before the narrator could light the candle.
   B ☐ after the narrator lit the candle.
   C ☐ because the room was too cold.
   D ☐ because Visger was in the bed.

5 The dead man in the hotel bed was
   A ☐ Visger.
   B ☐ a hallucination.
   C ☐ in the wrong room.
   D ☐ in his own room.

'If I see him again, I'll kill myself'

Remember that the first conditional is formed by two clauses.
The order of the clauses is not usually important:
If + present tense,   will + verb

- When the verb in the 'if' clause is negative (if ... not) we can also use **unless** and a **positive** verb:
  *If you **don't** light the candle, **he'll** come to me in the dark.*
  ***Unless** you **light** the candle, **he'll** come to me in the dark.*

- We may also use **can** or **must** in first conditional sentences:
  *If you **can** talk to me, you **won't** imagine things.*
  *Haldane **must** go to the doctor **if** he **feels** ill again.*

2 The first conditional

Complete these conditional sentences with the verbs in the correct form.

1 Haldane .... *(feel)* better if he goes travelling with his friend.
2 If the narrator can find the matches, he .... *(light)* the candle.
3 If Haldane .... *(drink)* some water, he won't be thirsty.
4 'You .... *(not get)* better unless you .... *(forget)* about Visger,' said the narrator.
5 Haldane said, 'I .... *(be)* safe if you .... *(not know)* where the body is.'
6 If his nerves .... *(be)* disturbed, Haldane .... *(must)* see a doctor.
7 Unless the narrator .... *(sleeps)* in the armchair in the hotel room, there .... *(be)* nowhere for him to sleep.

3 **Complete the following conditional sentences in your own words.**

1 The narrator and Haldane will see the Eiffel Tower if
....
2 .... unless the narrator helps him.
3 '.. in the dark, maybe I'll walk into something,' said Haldane.
4 If the narrator can light the candle in time, ...
....

67

4 Vocabulary

Complete the sentences with the adjectives in the box.

| pale | heavy | comfortable | untidy | thirsty | hard | full |

1   Haldane said the body on the carpet was ...., and also ...., like stone.

2   The narrator tried to sleep in the armchair, but it was not very ....

3   In Bruges the hotels were .... because there was an exhibition.

4   Haldane was ...., so he wanted some water.

5   Haldane sat up in bed, his hair .... and his face very ....

PET **5 Writing**

A friend of yours has invited you to stay at his/her flat in London.
In about 35-45 words write a card to send to your friend. In your card:

· thank him/her for the invitation;
· say why you would like to come;
· suggest a time in the future when you could come.

6 Who were these men in the story and what did they die of?

1   The man in bed in the hotel in Bruges.

2   The man on the train.

3   The men in the boxes left by Haldane.

7 At the beginning of the story the narrator's words are:

'Maybe he was mad. Maybe he had a sixth sense. Or was he really haunted?'

How would you explain what happened to Haldane? Compare your ideas in small groups.

The Versailles Ghosts

On 10 August 1901 two women were walking in the gardens of the Versailles Palace, near Paris. Eleanor Jourdain and Charlotte Moberly were well-educated English tourists in their thirties. Eleanor had a school for girls in Paris, and Charlotte was the principal of an Oxford college. They were not the kind of people who invent strange stories.

It was a fine day. The women were going to visit the famous Petit Trianon, a house built in the eighteenth century by Louis XV, the king of France from 1715-74. They came to a small path that went through some trees. As they walked along, everything became still and silent, and the two women felt as if they were walking in a dream. They felt a sad and heavy atmosphere all around them. Suddenly they saw two men dressed in green coats and hats of the eighteenth century. They looked like gardeners. The women asked them where the Petit Trianon was, and the men gave them directions.

After a while Eleanor saw two women in eighteenth century clothes. Then both women saw a man in a cloak [1] near a small summer house, [2] but he did not see them. They then asked another man in eighteenth century clothes where the Petit Trianon was, he told them the way and ran away. The women went across a little bridge near a waterfall. When they arrived at the garden behind the Petit Trianon, Charlotte saw a young woman wearing elegant clothes. She was sitting on a seat and drawing, and she looked at them as they passed.

---

1. **cloak** : a type of coat without sleeves.
2. **summer house** : a small building in a park or garden with seats.

At that moment a young man came out of the Petit Trianon, took them through the house, and left quickly. When they came out at the front of the house, the women saw that everything was normal again. The women began to think something strange had happened to them, and decided that the Petit Trianon was haunted.

Eleanor went back to Versailles in January 1902. She felt the same strange atmosphere. She saw the summer house, the bridge, and two workmen putting sticks in a cart. She heard voices, and sounds of silk dresses moving around her. Charlotte returned with Eleanor on 4 July 1904. This time everything was different: they could not find the path, and the summer house and bridge were not there. The place looked more modern.

Did the women see the Petit Trianon as it was in the summer of 1789? After some research they believed that the young woman in elegant clothes sitting in the garden was Marie Antoinette, the queen of France from 1774-93. The two gardeners were the Bersey brothers, who were working there at that time. The women also learnt that on 5 October 1789, after the French Revolution had begun, the French queen was sitting at the Petit Trianon, when she heard that thousands of angry people were walking towards the palace.

They wrote a book about their experience, *An Adventure*, which was published in 1911. The book created great public interest, selling 18,000 copies by 1913. Many people did not believe the story and thought the two women had lost their way, or were mistaken in remembering what they saw. One critic, W. H. Salter, who was a member of the Society of Psychical Research, said that the women did a lot of historical research for their book to make their story believable. The story of the 'Versailles ghosts' still remains a mystery.

The Petit Trianon at Versailles.

1 Tick (✓) the correct answer (A, B or C).

1 What happened on the path?

A ☐ The atmosphere changed.
B ☐ The women began to dream.
C ☐ The women saw the Petit Trianon.

2 Who saw the man in the cloak?

A ☐ Eleanor
B ☐ Charlotte
C ☐ Eleanor and Charlotte

3 Charlotte saw an elegant young woman

    A ☐ standing in the garden.

    B ☐ drawing something.

    C ☐ on the bridge.

4 In 1904

    A ☐ Eleanor returned to Versailles alone.

    B ☐ strange things happened again.

    C ☐ the scene was not the same as in 1901.

5 *An Adventure* was

    A ☐ an account of the women's supernatural experience.

    B ☐ not a success.

    C ☐ published soon after the events at Versailles.

 INTERNET PROJECT

The Palace of Versailles

Connect to the Internet and go to www.blackcat-cideb.com or www.cideb.it Insert the title or part of the title of the book into our search engine.

Open the page for *Tales of the Supernatural*. Click on the Internet project link. Go down the page until you find the title of this book and click on the relevant link for this project.

Find about the Palace of Versailles.

▶ How was it used in the past? What is it used for now?

▶ Who has lived there?

▶ What important historical events have taken place there?

Organise your class into two groups, A and B. Each group has to imagine the ways the palace can be used in the future. What can be done to attract visitors? Pairs made up of students from groups A and B compare their ideas.

The Upper Berth

F. Marion **Crawford**

Before you read

1 Vocabulary

The story is called 'The Upper Berth'. Do you know what this means? Only one of the definitions (1-3) is correct. Choose the correct definition.

1   The flat on the highest floor of a building.
2   The most expensive seating area in a theatre.
3   The top bed on a boat or train.

Look at the illustration on page 77 to check.

2 Pictures

Look again at the illustration on page 77.

1   Describe the men you can see in the illustration.
2   Where do you think the men are?
3   Do you think they know each other? Why/Why not?

3 Listening

Listen to the beginning of the story and decide if the statements 1-6 are true (T) or false (F).

		T	F
1	Brisbane was travelling to America on his favourite ship.	☐	☐
2	Brisbane was surprised because the steward on the ship was drunk.	☐	☐
3	The steward did not seem to like cabin 105.	☐	☐
4	Brisbane did not want to have another passenger in the cabin.	☐	☐
5	Brisbane thought the man in his cabin looked honest.	☐	☐
6	During the night Brisbane heard a noise and jumped from his bed.	☐	☐

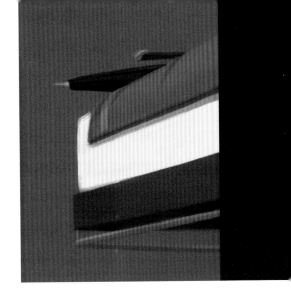

The Mystery of Cabin 105

e were all tired after a long dinner one evening, but nobody wanted to go home. Then somebody shouted, 'Bring the cigars!' It was Brisbane — a big, strong man. Everybody turned to look at him.

Lighting his cigar, he said, 'It's strange, you know.' We all stopped talking. 'It's strange,' he said again. 'People are always asking if anyone's seen a ghost. Well, I have.'

Somebody said, 'Tell us the story, Brisbane.' We lit our cigars, ordered another bottle of champagne, and listened to his story.

'When I used to travel to America, I liked to sail on certain ships. *The Kamtschatka* used to be my favourite. It isn't my favourite now, and I never want to travel on it again.

'I remember it was a warm morning in June. When I went on

board I told the steward [1] the number of my cabin — 105. He nearly dropped my suitcase.

'"Well, God help you!" he said quietly.

'I thought he might be drunk, but I said nothing and followed him. Cabin 105 was a large room with two berths with curtains around them. Mine was the lower one. That morning the cabin seemed empty and depressing, and I didn't like it.

'I gave the steward some money and he thanked me. "I'll try to make you comfortable," he said, and then added quietly, "If that's possible in this cabin."

'I was surprised, but again I thought he was drunk. I was wrong.

'Our voyage [2] began. On the first day everything was normal. That night I was tired and went to my cabin early. I noticed another suitcase by the door and a walking stick and an umbrella in the berth above mine. I wasn't happy because I had wanted to be on my own. Who was my companion? I decided to stay awake and see. Later, I was lying in bed in the dark when he came in. He was tall, very thin and pale, with fair hair and a beard and grey eyes. He looked like the type of man who makes money on Wall Street [3] or by gambling. I decided I didn't want to talk to him.

'"If he gets up early, I'll get up late," I said to myself before I went to sleep.

'During the night a loud noise suddenly woke me up. It was the other man jumping out of bed. Then I heard him unlock the cabin door; he ran out very fast, leaving the door open. I heard

1. **steward** : a person who looks after passengers on a ship.
2. **voyage** : a long journey by ship.
3. **Wall Street** : the financial area of New York City.

his footsteps along the passage. I got up angrily to close the door, and went back to sleep.

'When I woke up, it was still dark. The air was damp [1] and I felt cold. There was a strange smell in the cabin, like old sea water. I could hear the other man moving in the berth above mine. "So he's come back," I thought. Then he made a low sound of pain, and I thought he was feeling seasick. Then I fell asleep.

'When I woke up again the cabin was still cold. Suddenly I noticed that the window was open, so I got up and closed it. The curtains were closed around the other berth, so I thought the man was asleep. The smell of sea water had disappeared.

'At about seven o'clock I went for a walk around the ship and I met the ship's doctor from Ireland, a young man with black hair, blue eyes and a happy face. I said the weather was not very good.

'"It was very cold last night," I continued. "But my window was open all night, and the room was damp."

'"Damp! Where is your cabin?"

'"It's cabin 105…"

'The ship's doctor looked at me with big eyes. I asked what was the matter.

'"Oh — nothing,' he answered. "Well, I'll tell you. Everybody has complained about that room on our last three trips."

'"Good. And I'm going to complain, too."

'"But I believe there's something… No, I mustn't frighten you."

'"Oh, you won't frighten me. If I get a bad cold, I'll come to you!"

---

1. **damp** : slightly wet.

'We laughed, and I offered him a cigar. Then he asked me if I had a room-mate. [1]

'"Yes, a strange man who runs out in the middle of the night and leaves the door open."

'The ship's doctor gave me a curious look. "Did he come back?"

'"Yes. He was there when I woke up."

'"Look, my cabin is big enough for four people. You can sleep there tonight.' I was really surprised; why was he so anxious about me? I thanked him and said my cabin was fine: there was nothing wrong with it.

'"We doctors aren't superstitious," he said, "but please don't sleep in 105. Come and stay in my cabin."

'"But why?"

'"Because the last three people who slept there went overboard." [2]

'I looked at him to see if he was joking, but he looked very serious.

'I said, "I really don't think I'll be the fourth person to go overboard."

'"I think you'll change your mind before we arrive in America," he said.

'After breakfast I went to my cabin to get a book. The curtains around my room-mate's berth were still closed, so I thought he was asleep. As I came out, I met the steward, who said the captain wanted to see me in his cabin.

---

1. **room-mate** : someone who shares a room or cabin with you.
2. **went overboard** : jumped or fell into the sea.

"'I want to ask you a favour,' said the captain when I arrived. "Your room-mate has disappeared. Did you notice anything strange about him?"

"'Has he… gone overboard?" I asked, remembering the ship doctor's story.

"'Yes, I think so."

"'That's incredible! He's the fourth person." And I told him the story of cabin 105. I also told him what had happened to me in the night.

"'That's the same story the other room-mates told me," the captain said. "Nobody saw the man last night. The steward found his berth empty this morning and looked for him, but he's disappeared. Please don't tell the other passengers. I don't want my ship to get a bad reputation for suicide. You can sleep in any cabin you like for the rest of the voyage. Is that alright?"

"'Thank you, Captain, but my cabin is empty now so I'll stay there."

'The captain tried to change my mind, but I told him I was happy to have the room to myself. I asked him if the steward could remove my room-mate's things and do something about the damp and the window. After I left the captain, I saw the ship's doctor and we played cards. I went to my room late.'

Go back to the text

1 Summing it up

Put the sentences A-J in the correct order to make a summary of Chapter One. Write 1-10 in the boxes.

A ☐ Then Brisbane woke up again and noticed that the cabin was cold, damp, and smelt of old sea water.

B ☐ So Brisbane told the captain about the cabin and what happened in the night.

C ☐ On board, the steward seemed so strange about cabin 105 that Brisbane thought he was drunk.

D ☐ After breakfast, Brisbane spoke to the captain, who said Brisbane's room-mate had probably jumped overboard.

E ☐ About 7 a.m. he met the ship's doctor on deck and told him about his strange night.

F ☐ One June morning Brisbane embarked on *The Kamtschatka* to sail to America.

G ☐ That night Brisbane woke up when the other passenger in the cabin jumped from his bed and ran out.

H ☐ And in the morning he saw that the window was open.

I ☐ Finally, Brisbane asked the captain if the steward could do something about the damp and the window.

J ☐ The doctor said the last three passengers in cabin 105 went overboard.

PET 2 Read the text below and choose the correct word for each space. For each question, write the letter A, B, C or D, as in the example (0).

Brisbane sailed (**0**) ...B............. America in June on board *The Kamtschatka*. His cabin was number 105. When the steward (**1**) .... this, he acted strangely, and Brisbane (**2**) .... he was drunk. That night Brisbane noticed that there was (**3**) .... passenger in the cabin. He was not happy about this because he wanted to be (**4**) .... While he was in bed, a tall, thin man came in. Brisbane did not like his appearance. (**5**) .... the night Brisbane

woke up and saw the man run out of the cabin. Later, he woke up
(6) .... cold. The air in the cabin was damp, and there was
(7) .... strange smell of old sea water. The other passenger
(8) .... in bed and (9) .... to be in pain.

0	**A** about	**B** to	**C** at	**D** out
1	**A** found	**B** heard	**C** remembered	**D** asked
2	**A** prayed	**B** looked	**C** thought	**D** talked
3	**A** other	**B** others	**C** another	**D** more
4	**A** own	**B** alone	**C** one	**D** lonely
5	**A** During	**B** After	**C** At	**D** By
6	**A** being	**B** having	**C** wanting	**D** feeling
7	**A** one	**B** the	**C** its	**D** a
8	**A** was	**B** had	**C** has	**D** is
9	**A** seemed	**B** sounded	**C** cried	**D** shouted

'I told the steward that the number of my cabin was 105'

Remember in reported statements the verb tense changes. In this
sentence Brisbane is reporting what he said to the steward.
*Brisbane said to the steward, 'The number of my cabin **is** 105.'*
Note the changes in this example of a reported question:
The ship's doctor asked, 'Have you got a room-mate?'
*The ship's doctor asked if I **had** a room-mate.*
Note that 'got' is not necessary with 'had'.

3 Reported statements and questions
**Can you change these reported statements and questions using the
words spoken?**

1   I said the weather was not very good.
    I said, '... .'
2   I told the captain there was something wrong with cabin 105.
    I said to the captain, '... .'
3   The steward said my suitcase was heavy.
    '... ,' said the steward.

4   The doctor asked Brisbane if he was in cabin 105.
    '..?' the doctor asked Brisbane.
5   Brisbane asked the captain if he knew the story about cabin 105.
    '..?' Brisbane asked.

④ Now change the following to reported statements and questions.

1   'My cabin is big enough for four people,' said the doctor.
    The doctor said ....
2   I said to the ship's doctor, 'My room-mate has got fair hair and a beard.' I told ....
3   'Do you want to sleep in my cabin?' the ship's doctor asked me.
    ....
4   'Have we got any cigars?' Brisbane asked.
    ....
5   'Are you joking?' I asked the doctor.
    ....

PET ⑤ Brisbane saw these notices around the ship. Look at the text in each question. What does it say? Tick (✓) the correct box (A, B or C).

1

No passengers beyond this point

A ☐ Passengers can go further than the notice.

B ☐ Passengers are not allowed to go further than the notice.

C ☐ Passengers must not walk near the notice.

2

IN CASE OF EMERGENCY PLEASE ASSEMBLE ON DECK E

A ☐ Don't meet on Deck E if there is an emergency.

B ☐ Unless there is an emergency, meet on Deck E.

C ☐ If there is an emergency, passengers must meet on Deck E.

3

8.00 tonight
dinner & dance.
Formal dress required.

A ☐ Passengers can wear T-shirts.

B ☐ Passengers can't wear jeans and trainers.

C ☐ Passengers must wear dresses.

4

MESSAGE SERVICE:
Mr Brisbane. Steward will
leave key to your cabin at
reception on Deck A.

Where is the key now?

A ☐ In cabin 105.

B ☐ At reception on Deck A.

C ☐ With the steward.

Before you read

1 Listening

Read sentences 1-8. You will hear the beginning of Chapter Two. For each question, fill in the missing information in the spaces.

1 The frightened steward closed the window and asked Brisbane to check if ....

2 Then the steward said, 'You'll see that in half an hour it .... and secured, too.'

3 '...,' Brisbane replied, 'I'll give you £10.'

4 Later, as Brisbane ...., he suddenly felt some cold air and sea water on his face.

5 Jumping out of bed, he noticed that the window was open — .... !

6 Then he heard a sound from the bed, so he opened the curtain and touched ....

7 A soft, wet, heavy thing came towards him and ....

8 The door opened and the thing .... cabin into the corridor, where it disappeared.

CHAPTER **TWO**

The Cabin of Terror

n my cabin I thought of the tall man, now dead somewhere in the ocean, and I opened the curtains around his berth. It was empty. Suddenly I noticed that the window was open and secured [1] with a hook. [2] Angry, I went to look for the steward. I showed him the window.

'"Why is it open?" I shouted. "I'll report you to the captain."

'The steward was frightened and he closed the window. "Nobody can keep this window closed at night, sir. Look, is that locked or not? You try it and see, please."

'The window was securely locked.

'"Well, you'll see that in half an hour it'll be open again — and secured, too. That's the horrible thing, sir — it is secured with the hook!"

---

1. **secured** : fixed firmly in place.   2. **hook** :

'I checked the window again. "If I find it open in the night, I'll give you ten pounds. But it's impossible."

'We said goodnight, and I went to bed. I tried to sleep, but I couldn't. Sometimes I looked at the window; it was closed, and I smiled thinking of the steward's story. As I was falling asleep, I suddenly felt some cold air and sea water on my face. I jumped out of bed, and the movement of the ship threw me onto the sofa under the window. It was open — and secured with the hook! I was surprised but not scared. I closed the window and locked it. Then I stood watching it in the dark cabin.

'Suddenly I heard a sound behind me and turned round. A sound of pain came from the berth above mine. I opened the curtain and put my hand in: there was somebody in it! The air was very damp, and there was a horrible smell of old sea water. I touched a man's arm; it was wet, and as cold as ice. As I pulled it, the thing came towards me — a soft, wet, heavy thing — and it fell against me. I fell back across the cabin. In a moment the door opened and the thing ran out. I followed it as fast as possible. I'm sure I saw it in the low light of the corridor before it disappeared. Now I was really frightened.

'"This is crazy," I thought. Had I really seen it? I went back into the cabin, lit a candle and saw with horror that the window was open. I looked at the other berth; it smelt of sea water but it was dry! I closed the window and sat on the sofa all night. The window did not open.

'When dawn came, I got dressed and went on deck, where I saw the ship's doctor.

'"You were right, Doctor," I said. "There's something very strange about cabin 105."

'"Did you have a bad night?" he asked.

'So I told him everything. Then I asked if he believed me.

'"Yes, of course. You must come and stay in my cabin tonight."

'"Why don't you come and stay in mine for one night? Help me to understand what happened."

'"I'm sorry, but no. I don't want to see any ghosts."

'I laughed at him. "Do you really believe it was a ghost?"

'"Can you explain it then?" he asked angrily. "No, you can't!"

'"But you're a doctor, a man of science. You must know there's a rational explanation."

'"There isn't a rational explanation. I hope you find somebody to help you. Good morning, Mr Brisbane." And the ship's doctor continued his walk.

'I didn't want to spend another night in my cabin, but I was obstinate and decided to do it alone. I couldn't find anybody to help me. Later, I met the captain and told him this.

'"I'll stay with you tonight," he said, "and we'll see what happens. I think we can find out what's wrong with that berth.'

'He brought a carpenter [1] to the cabin and told him to examine the berth very carefully. When the carpenter finished his work he said, "In my opinion it's better to lock the door with some big screws. [2] Four people have died already. This cabin is haunted."

'"I'll try it for one more night," I answered.

'I was feeling better now because I had the captain's company for the night. He was a calm, brave man, and he really wanted to

---

1. **carpenter** : a person who makes things from wood.

2. **screws** :

solve the mystery. I was smoking a cigar at about ten o'clock that evening when he came to speak to me.

"'This is a serious problem, Mr Brisbane," he said. "We've lost four passengers on four trips, so we must find out what's wrong. If nothing happens tonight, we'll try tomorrow. Are you ready?"

'We went down to cabin 105. The captain closed the door and locked it. He put my big suitcase in front of the door and sat on it, so nothing could get out. The window was closed. I opened the curtains around the other berth, and put my lamp there. Then I checked around the cabin and under my bed and the sofa.

"'Nobody can come into the cabin, nobody can open the window, and only you and I are in the cabin," I said.

"'Very good," answered the captain calmly. "So if we see anything, it's only our imagination — or something supernatural."

"'Do you really believe it's something supernatural?" I asked sleepily.

"'No, I don't. What are you looking at?"

'I didn't answer. I was looking at the window; was the lock really beginning to turn or was it my imagination? Yes, perhaps it was — very slowly, so slowly that I wasn't really sure.

"'It's moving!" the captain cried. "But what's that smell? I can smell old sea water — can you?"

"'Yes. It's strange because the cabin is dry," I said.

Just then my lamp suddenly went out. As I stood up to get it, the captain jumped up with a loud cry of surprise. I turned and ran towards him as he called for help. He was trying to stop the window from opening, but the lock was turning against his hands. Suddenly the window opened. The captain, his face very pale, stood by the door so nobody could escape.

'"There's somebody in that berth!" he shouted, his eyes big and scared. "Stand by the door while I look. It won't escape."

'But I jumped up and put my hands into the upper berth. Inside there was something ghostly and horrible, and it moved in my hands. It felt like the body of a drowned [1] man — cold, soft, and wet from a long time in the water. I held on to it tightly but it was as strong as ten men. And it moved, a smooth, wet thing with a putrid [2] smell, and dead white eyes that stared at me, and wet hair over its dead face. It pushed against me, put its arms around my neck, and forced me back. I fought with the thing, but it was too strong, and finally I fell and let it go.

'It moved quickly towards the captain. He tried to hit it, but he fell down with a cry of horror. As the thing stood over the captain, I almost screamed with terror, but I had no voice. Suddenly the thing disappeared. It seemed to go through the window, but I don't know how that was possible.

'The captain and I lay on the floor for a long time. When I moved at last, I knew my arm was broken. I stood up and tried to help the captain; he wasn't injured, but he was in a bad state of shock.

'That's the end of my story. The ship's carpenter put four big screws in the door of 105, and no passengers slept in it again. If you ever travel on *The Kamtschatka* and ask for that cabin, the captain will tell you that it's occupied. Yes, it is occupied — by a dead thing!'

---

1. **drowned** : died underwater.
2. **putrid** : something with a strong smell because it has become bad.

Go back to the text

1 Summing it up

Match the first half of each sentence (1-8) to the second half (A-H) to make a summary of Chapter Two. Write A-H in the boxes.

1 ☐ After the steward locked the window, Brisbane checked it
2 ☐ But that night the window opened again, and Brisbane
3 ☐ The next night Brisbane and the captain went to the cabin,
4 ☐ After a while, they smelt an odour of old sea water
5 ☐ Then Brisbane tried to fight with a wet, dead thing in the upper berth
6 ☐ It went to the door, where the captain tried to hit it
7 ☐ Terrified, Brisbane watched the thing
8 ☐ Afterwards, a carpenter put four big screws in the cabin door

A locked the door and the window, and waited.
B and nobody slept in it again.
C and saw that the window was opening.
D but fell down with a cry of horror.
E had a frightening encounter with a horrible thing in the upper berth.
F as it seemed to disappear through the window.
G and went to bed.
H but it was too strong for him.

PET 2 Language

Here are some sentences from Chapter Two. Complete the second sentence so that it means the same as the first. Use no more than three words.

Example: The ghost was stronger than Brisbane.
          Brisbane .....wasn't as.............. strong as the ghost.

1   There was a smell of old sea water in the berth.
    The berth .... of old sea water.
2   The lamp in the corridor gave only a little light.
    The lamp in the corridor didn't give ....
3   Cabin 105 is occupied by a dead thing.
    A dead thing .... cabin 105.
4   'I'll stay with you for the night,' said the captain.
    The captain offered .... Brisbane for the night.

3 Picture summary

Put the pictures below in the correct order to make a picture summary of Chapter Two. Write 1-6 in the boxes.

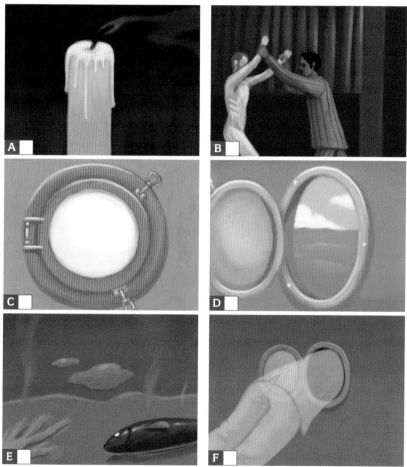

 ### 4 Writing

You are going on a voyage by sea. Write an email of about 35-45 words to a friend. In your email you should:

- say where you are sailing to;
- explain why you are going;
- say how long you will be away;
- arrange to meet your friend when you return.

1 **Which of the people (A-J) in the stories do the questions 1-10 refer to? Write A-J in the boxes.**

A	The signalman	**F**	The narrator of 'Ligeia'
B	The ghost in 'The Signalman'	**G**	Lady Rowena
C	Haldane	**H**	Brisbane
D	Visger	**I**	The dead thing in 'The Upper Berth'
E	Ligeia	**J**	The captain

Who ...

1. ☐ was a clever student of languages?
2. ☐ was worried about the reputation of his ship?
3. ☐ told Haldane's girlfriend bad things about him?
4. ☐ loved his first wife more than his second wife?
5. ☐ always appeared at the red light?
6. ☐ was as strong as ten men?
7. ☐ obstinately refused to sleep in another cabin?
8. ☐ could not understand the ghost's warning?
9. ☐ loved a girl who died suddenly?
10. ☐ died and changed into somebody very different?

2 **Read the text and answer the questions. Decide if the statements are true (T) or false (F). Tick (✓) the correct box.**

On 5 October 1869 a very strange thing happened in Highgate Cemetery, London. This cemetery had a bad reputation. People said it was one of the most haunted places in London. The scene on that autumn night was like something from a macabre tale by Edgar Allan Poe.

Some men were opening the grave of a woman called Elizabeth Siddall. In 1862, when she died at the age of twenty-nine, her husband was very sad. He was the poet and painter Dante Gabriel Rossetti, and to show his great love for his wife he put the only complete manuscript of his poems in her coffin. In her life Elizabeth was his favourite model. She appears in many of his paintings. Her hair was very long, and had a beautiful red-gold colour.

For the next seven years Rossetti was haunted by the memory of his beautiful wife. Then in 1869 his agent, Charles Augustus Howell, persuaded him to open Elizabeth's grave and take out the poems. Howell wanted Rossetti to publish the 'book from the grave' and make some money. An enormous bonfire lit up the cold, damp night. In the light of the fire Rossetti saw that Elizabeth's hair was still a beautiful red-gold colour. And it was much longer than in 1862 when she was buried!

The volume of *Poems* was published in 1870. But critics attacked the book. Rossetti became physically and mentally ill, and tried to commit suicide in 1872. Ten years later he died, a sick, lonely man. Was the ghost of his wife angry with him for taking the poems from her grave?

		T	F
1	People believed that Highgate Cemetery was haunted.	☐	☐
2	The events happened in the autumn of 1862.	☐	☐
3	Elizabeth Siddall was young when she died.	☐	☐
4	Rossetti buried the poems with his wife as a sign of his love for her.	☐	☐
5	Elizabeth had beautiful, long hair.	☐	☐
6	Rossetti forgot about his wife after her death.	☐	☐
7	Rossetti took the poems because he wanted to sell them.	☐	☐
8	There was a large bonfire on Elizabeth Siddall's grave.	☐	☐
9	When she was buried Elizabeth's hair was shorter than in 1869.	☐	☐

Key to Exit Test
1 1F 2J 3D 4F 5B 6F 7H 8A 9C 10C
2 1T 2F 3T 4F 5T 6F 7T 8F 9F

This reader uses the **EXPANSIVE READING** approach, where the text becomes a springboard to improve language skills and to explore historical background, cultural connections and other topics suggested by the text. The new structures introduced in this step of our **READING & TRAINING** series are listed below. Naturally, structures from lower steps are included, too. For a complete list of structures used over all the six steps, see *The Black Cat Guide to Graded Readers*, which is also downloadable at no cost from our website, www.blackcat-cideb.com or www.cideb.it. The vocabulary used at each step is carefully checked against vocabulary lists used for internationally recognised examinations.

Step Three B1.2

All the structures used in the previous levels, plus the following:

Verb tenses
Present Perfect Simple: unfinished past with *for* or *since* (duration form)
Past Perfect Simple: narrative

Verb forms and patterns
Regular verbs and all irregular verbs in current English
Causative: *have / get* + object + past participle
Reported questions and orders with *ask* and *tell*

Modal verbs
Would: hypothesis
Would rather: preference
Should (present and future reference): moral obligation
Ought to (present and future reference): moral obligation
Used to: past habits and states

Types of clause
2nd Conditional: *if* + past, *would(n't)*
Zero, 1st and 2nd conditionals with *unless*
Non-defining relative clauses with *who* and *where*
Clauses of result: *so*; *so ... that*; *such ... that*
Clauses of concession: *although, though*

Other
Comparison: *(not) as / so ... as*; *(not) ... enough to*; *too ... to*

Available at Step Three:

- **The £1,000,000 Banknote** Mark Twain
- **The Canterville Ghost** Oscar Wilde
- **Classic Detective Stories**
- **The Diamond as Big as The Ritz** F. Scott Fitzgerald
- **Great Mysteries of Our World** Gina D. B. Clemen
- **Gulliver's Travels** Jonathan Swift
- **The Hound of the Baskervilles** Sir Arthur Conan Doyle
- **Jane Eyre** Charlotte Brontë
- **Julius Caesar** William Shakespeare
- **Kim** Rudyard Kipling
- **Lord Arthur Savile's Crime and Other Stories** Oscar Wilde
- **Moonfleet** John Meade Falkner
- **Of Mice and Men** John Steinbeck
- **The Pearl** John Steinbeck
- **The Phantom of the Opera** Gaston Leroux
- **The Prisoner of Zenda** Anthony Hope
- **The Return of Sherlock Holmes** Sir Arthur Conan Doyle
- **Romeo and Juliet** William Shakespeare
- **The Scarlet Pimpernel** Baroness Orczy
- **Sherlock Holmes Investigates** Sir Arthur Conan Doyle
- **Stories of Suspense** Nathaniel Hawthorne
- **The Strange Case of Dr Jekyll and Mr Hyde** Robert Louis Stevenson
- **Tales of the Supernatural**
- **Three Men in a Boat** Jerome K. Jerome
- **Treasure Island** Robert Louis Stevenson
- **True Adventure Stories** Peter Foreman
- **Twelfth Night** William Shakespeare

R&T *Discovery*
- **American Cities** Gina D. B. Clemen